BETHLEHEM LUTHERAN LIBRARY

Candles in the Night

Publishing House
St. Louis

Frederick A. Radtke

Thirty-One Meditations for Persons Called by God to Bring Up a Handicapped Child

Candles in the Night

Unless otherwise stated, Scripture quotations are used by permission of American Bible Society, from THE GOOD NEWS BIBLE, Copyright © TEV, 1966, 1971, 1976.

All rights reserved. No portion of this book may be reproduced in any form whatsoever, except for brief quotations in reviews, without the written pemission of the publisher.

Concordia Publishing House, St. Louis, Missouri

Copyright © 1978 Concordia Publishing House

Manufactured in the United States of America

Library of Congress Cataloging in Pubication Date

Radtke, Frederick A., 1926-
    Candles in the night.

    1. Meditations. 2. Mentally handicapped children. 3. Family—Prayer-books and devotions—English. I. Title
BV4845.R32   242'.4   78-1937
ISBN 0-570-03776-X

With these meditations
the author,
himself the father
of a handicapped child,
has attempted to move
parents of a newborn
handicapped infant
from shock to shell;
that is,
from the shock of having
a handicapped offspring
to the shell of God's grace
that all people
have in Jesus
their Savior
through Baptism.

This book is dedicated to Martin

Contents

God Has Given You a Child to Love	Ephesians 6:14-18	9
Loads Made Light	Luke 11:46	12
Proof of the Spirit's Presence	1 Corinthians 12:4-7	14
Using the Power of Christ	Philippians 3:20-21	17
Tottering Steps of Faith	Psalm 126:2-3	19
Lord, to Whom Would We Go?	John 6:66-69	21
Tedium to Te Deum	John 10:17-18	23
Be Not Afraid; It Is I	Luke 12:7	25
The Sum of the Parts	1 Corinthians 12:12-27	27
Recalled to Life	John 10:27-28	30
The Message of God's Hope	Luke 24:5b	32
No Idle Coincidence	Isaiah 44:1-2	34
Hidden Resources	Luke 12:48b	36
Love That Endures	1 Corinthians 13:4-8	38
Face to Face	1 Corinthians 13:11-13	40
A Life Controlled by Love	Ephesians 4:31—5:2	42
Service That Never Loses Its Value	1 Corinthians 15:50-58	44
Many from One	John 12:24-26	47
Moving with Hope	John 10:2-5	49
To Be Born Again	John 3:4-7	52
Strengthened Through Prayer	Luke 22:32	55
Rejected Stones	Luke 20:17-18	58
First Let Me Go	Luke 9:59-62	60
So That God's Power May Be Seen	John 9:1-5	63
An Invitation to Love	Luke 9:23-26	65
How Happy to Have No Doubts	Luke 7:22-23	68
Prophet, Priest, and King	Luke 4:18-19	71
Provided with All Things	Matthew 6:32b-34	73
The Glory That Is Going to Be	1 Peter 5:8-11	75
As I Have Loved You	Luke 17:9-10	77
Clay Pots or Flower Vases?	2 Corinthians 4:7—5:2	79
Postscript		83

God Has Given You a Child to Love

"The sun was shining; it was a beautiful day . . . a beautiful day after the delivery. As I lay in my hospital bed, the morning began to drag. It seemed that the other mothers on the floor had already received their babies. Yet, the doctor hadn't been around. Probably our baby . . . my baby . . . would soon be brought in. And sure enough. Not only was my baby brought in, but Dr. Brown brought him in himself along with Bill, my husband, and Pastor Williams."

Pastor Williams began rather slowly: "Good morning, Mrs. Reynolds. This is a special occasion, and Dr. Brown and I thought it would be wise that we all come together and have Bill here too. Dr. Brown and other doctors on the hospital staff want you to know their concern that the baby God has given you is a special child. He's special in many ways. From reliable observations the doctors believe the little fellow will need your additional attention and love to help him develop as much as possible to overcome his apparent present limited development."

Why do these things happen? We really don't know, and it really isn't important. What is important is that God has given you a child to hold and to love. Just as we know Jesus loved children, so we know God loves your infant too; for He gave it to Christian parents. As with all other newborn babies, you have the assurance that God has given you an opportunity to reach out to this redeemed child of God with the love that God has given you. We love Him because He first loved us.

This child that God has given you is an

opportunity to share God's grace with him. God has called you to a special witnessing of your faith. We know that bringing up a handicapped child is not always easy; it is not always enjoyable. In a real sense God is calling you to carry a cross that no one can say will be easy. But in a larger sense you can have the assurance of God's love for both you and your baby.

In asking any mother and father to accept this challenge, it is not only advisable but it is necessary to look to His holy Word.

St. Paul's words ring true for us now, and his words will remain a constant blessing to you in those days when your cross may burden you:

> So stand ready, with truth as a belt tight around your waist, with righteousness as your breastplate, and as your shoes the readiness to announce the Good News of peace. At all times carry faith as a shield; with it you will be able to put out all the burning arrows shot by the Evil One. And accept salvation as a helmet, and the word of God as the sword which the Spirit gives you. Do all this in prayer, asking for God's help. Pray on every occasion, as the Spirit leads. For this reason keep alert and never give up; pray always for all God's people *(Eph. 6:14-18).*

When parents of a handicapped child know Jesus as their Lord and Savior, they gain new spiritual insight and strength to bring up their child as one of God's children, an heir of eternal life in heaven. It is a fact that they are not alone, but that they stand together with all other Christian parents as called servants of the Most High God. When you hold this truth of God's Word in your heart through good days and seemingly bad days, you will be able to say with

Peter. "Lord, how good it is that we are here"; and later you will say, "We saw His glory, full of grace and truth. This was the glory which He received as the Father's only Son" *(John 1:14)*.

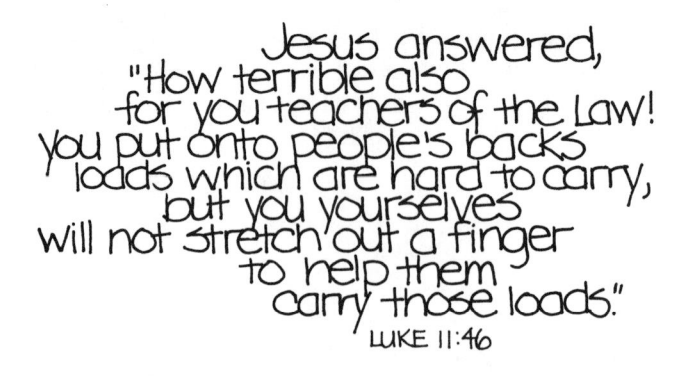

> Jesus answered, "How terrible also for you teachers of the Law! You put onto people's backs loads which are hard to carry, but you yourselves will not stretch out a finger to help them carry those loads."
>
> LUKE 11:46

Loads Made Light

Even as followers of Jesus are the children of God, the teachers of the Law in rejecting Jesus the Messiah are the children of the devil.

When people put loads of shame and guilt upon the backs of parents of a handicapped child, the parents should recognize the source of this evil.

Jesus speaks directly to the teachers of the Law, the Pharisees and the Sadducees. He warns them of the eternal punishment that threatens them because of their loveless and merciless attitude. He recognizes the fact that they refuse to become personally involved. Many people today too refuse to become personally involved in helping handicapped persons. They stand in a vertical relationship to them. They refuse to share one another's burdens in a personal, direct relationship. Like the priest and the Levite in the parable of the Good Samaritan, they walk by on the other side; for they are confronted with the presence of God Himself.

These loads are especially hard to carry because the world, the devil, and our own flesh would rob us of Christ's comforting message of God's free grace.

When Jesus encountered the man blind since birth, He told His disciples that neither this man nor his parents had sinned to cause him to be blind. When we parents of a handicapped child are assured that neither we nor our child are the cause of our child's handicap, but "that God's power might be seen at work," then our burden of guilt is removed and Christ's words, ". . . the load I will put on you is light," are fulfilled.

Loads of shame and guilt are not the cross that Jesus invites His followers to take up, but they are loads that are placed on people's backs without mercy or love. Followers of Jesus recognize their true cross in life and willingly take up that cross in Jesus' name. Under this true cross parents and other members of the family see the glory of the risen Lord, that Lord who conquered death and offers life and salvation to all who believe as the words and promise of God declare. In the shadow of that cross parents stand supported by God's love. In the shadow of that cross they recognize their own cross as an opportunity to grow in grace. Their whole life takes on a new perspective. The trying experiences of daily living become a blessing whereby they, like the children of Israel, shout with the shout of joy: "We will serve the Lord."

> There are different kinds of spiritual gifts, but the same spirit gives them. There are different ways of serving, but the same Lord is served. There are different abilities to perform service, but the same God gives ability to everyone for their particular service. The spirit's presence is shown in someway in each person for the good of all.
> 1 CORINTHIANS 12:4-7

Proof of the Spirit's Presence

The world thinks, "A wasted life," when it sees a handicapped person. Yet St. Paul reminds us that everyone (including the handicapped child) is given ability. Parents of a special child are not ready to assign such meager importance to serving their loved one. They know "a little child shall lead them" *(KJV)* They know that their child offers proof of the Spirit's presence for the good of all, that is, for the body of Christ, the communion of saints, the congregation of believers.

Yes, a little child shall lead them. "There are different ways of serving, but the same Lord is served." Glory be to Jesus that we can look beyond our service and see the different service of the handicapped. For it is not the service in itself that is important, but it is the heart of gratitude to God for sending His Son into the world to save us that is important. For this reason the gift of love a handicapped child offers shows forth the glory of God, for it is proof of the Spirit's presence for the good of all.

The blind English poet John Milton concluded, after losing his eyesight, "They also serve who only stand and wait." Is not this a service handicapped persons render? Yes, but is it enough? "When they are insulted, they do not answer back with an insult"; when pushed aside, denied the opportunity to serve in those capacities where they are able, handicapped persons have waited patiently; but is it sufficient to say that this is the limit of their service to their Lord and Savior?

One evening an autistic boy after being confirmed in church walked up the chancel steps and in the presence of the congregation said to his pastor, "I love you." "How beautiful are the feet of them that preach the Gospel of peace and bring glad tidings of good things!" *(KJV)*. That evening the congregation of believers who were present concluded with the two Emmaus disciples, "Did not our heart burn within us . . . ?" *(KJV)* An unsophisticated witness of faith, and we know that "we beheld His glory, the glory of the only-begotten . . . full of grace and truth" *(KJV)*.

Why are we here on earth? How can we serve? Can the handicapped person serve also? How happy the parents of the autistic boy could be! He had fulfilled God's word before them: "There are different kinds of spiritual gifts, but the same Spirit gives them. . . . There are different abilities to perform service, but the same God gives ability to everyone for their particular service. The Spirit's presence is shown in some way in each person." "A wasted life!" the world concludes, but parents of handicapped children cry back, "No!" There is a purpose for everyone. Handicapped persons can show the faith in their hearts; they can serve in different ways, and the greatest of these is to love.

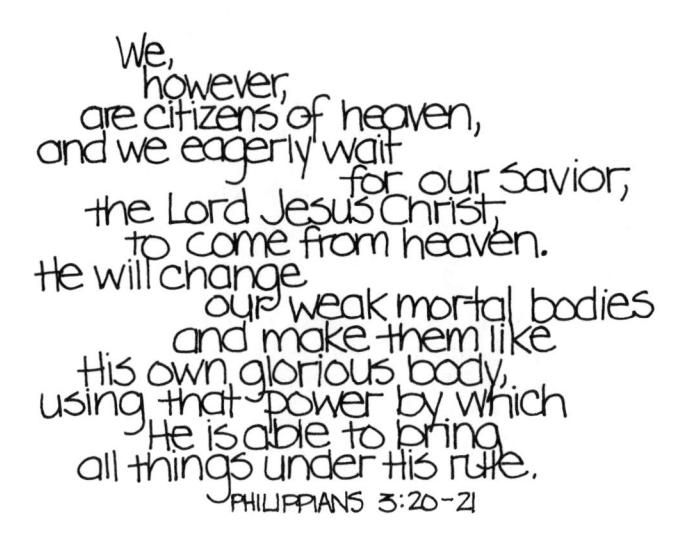

> We,
> however,
> are citizens of heaven,
> and we eagerly wait
> for our Savior,
> the Lord Jesus Christ,
> to come from heaven.
> He will change
> our weak mortal bodies
> and make them like
> His own glorious body,
> using that power by which
> He is able to bring
> all things under His rule.
>
> PHILIPPIANS 3:20-21

Using the Power of Christ

Jean Vanier, the world-renowned founder of the community residence l'Arche in Trosly-Breuil, France, questioned why humanity in general rejects handicapped persons, answered that people see in them their own destruction.

Edmund Schlink in his *Theology of the Lutheran Confessions* states:

> When the [handicapped person] confesses that God has given him "all limbs and senses, my reason and all faculties of my mind . . . and still sustains" them, he is confessing the Creator-Spirit who will give the new body and who makes this eschatological fact, now invisible to human eyes, more sure and more present than the mutilated visible reality of this world of sin and death.

No wonder the world becomes unsettled! No wonder the world becomes unnerved in the presence of the handicapped; for the world is reminded of its own judgment before God. But not so with the followers of Jesus Christ. As citizens of heaven they are reminded of the glorious resurrection which they and all Christians have already been promised and which they own not at some future day, but now.

This living hope motivates the family of a handicapped child to encircle the newborn infant in love, that same love of God through our Lord and Savior Jesus Christ that encircles them. In experiencing this love, the infant reaches out and reflects the glorious body we all shall wear with Christ.

When the presence of a handicapped person reminds parents of the sonship they have in Christ, they sense, beyond the reality of the child's earthly needs, the greater reality of the spiritual things that have to do with eternity. They trim their lamps of faith; they secure their own supply of oil for that day when Christ shall appear and change weak mortal bodies—not only their handicapped child's but also their own.

Praise be to God! Jesus Christ lives and reigns in His kingdom to all eternity. Not only parents but also handicapped children live under His rule as citizens of heaven.

Then was our mouth filled with laughter, and our tongue with singing: ...The Lord hath done great things for us; whereof we are glad.

PSALM 126:2-3 KJV

Tottering Steps of Faith

It is a delightful day in May; the relatives have gathered for a birthday party to celebrate your second son's first birthday. It is an occasion not easily forgotten. Perhaps it is the sense of something special, the excitement of tearing brightly colored paper from boxes filled with gifts. Perhaps it is the special attention that gives the birthday child the impetus to leave the security of holding on to the wooden chair and to venture out into space. With quick, tottering steps he falls forward into the waiting arms of Grandpa. He must try it again . . . and again . . . and again; each time a chorus of approval is emitted from his world of adults.

Then, into this scene comes the older brother, scooting along on his bottom; for he is handicapped, and he does not walk . . . yet. He senses the excitement; he sees the approval; he regards his younger brother with appreciation. Slowly he reaches up to take hold of the wooden chair. He pulls himself upward. He is standing. Slowly he moves his head to take in this new world. There is a quiet, perhaps tense, look about him. Grandpa is aware of this grandson's achievement, too. He holds out his arms. Slowly, hesitantly he tippy-toes into the arms of Grandpa.

Truly your joy as a parent or grandparent runneth over. Surely goodness and mercy shall follow you all the days of your life. Twice blessed are you. Even as your handicapped son modeled himself after his younger brother, in the same way, with the same wavering, tottering steps of faith you model your spiritual life after Christ, the Good Shepherd. You remember His words: "I will never leave thee nor forsake thee. . . . Lo, I am with you always" *(KJV)*. The joys of parenting a handicapped child are simple joys; they are the same joys that other parents experience, but they are the joys of patient waiting; they are the joys of battles won lately; they are joys sweetly won. "And we beheld His glory, the glory as of the only begotten of the Father, full of grace and truth" *(KJV)*. He gave us His Son—will He not also freely give us all things?"

> Because of this,
> many of Jesus' followers
> turned back and would not go
> with Him anymore.
> So He asked
> the twelve disciples,
> "And you—
> would you also like to leave?"
> Simon Peter answered him:
> "Lord, to whom would we go?
> You have the words
> that give eternal life.
> And now we believe
> and know
> that You are the Holy One
> who has come from God."
> JOHN 6:66-69

Lord, to Whom Would We Go?

A baby new-born is a sense of hope; here lies a new beginning. Psychologically, parents project a state of innocence, the possibility of perfection in human development. Confronted by these aspirations, parents of a newborn handicapped child in their dilemma are tested to turn away from Jesus. "If God is a God of mercy," they cry out, "why would He allow this to happen to us—we who are faithful followers of His?" But men's ways are not God's ways.

With God's help Christian parents of a handicapped child can grow in wisdom even as the vine does. In their attempt to synchronize their not-normal living routines with the structures of the world, they are cut back to the living vine. In losing credibility with the world, they verge on the brink of losing credibility with themselves. For such parents it is only through living life day by day over the expanse of years that the reality of God's wisdom becomes their own. In this eternity of time the fruit of patience permeates the parents' souls and they say with Peter, "Lord, to whom would we go?" Christ is the answer; there is no other. He is the "Why"; He is the Alpha and the Omega.

There are moments, there are days when we would "like to leave." But the Comforter is with us with His love. It is He who steadies our vision to look beyond our mundane existence and see, reflected in our tears, the joy of His peace. We remember Christ's words that give eternal salvation. Time is refracted; time loses its hold; the mansions of eternity come before our eyes. We believe; we know with certainty that Christ is the Holy One from God. We are one with Christ in His body and in His Spirit. He is the Fountain of refreshment and strength in our weakness. "Lord, to whom would we go? You have the words that give eternal life." That eternal life begins now. That eternal life begins in sadness, but our joy will be complete.

> The Father loves Me because I am willing to give up My life, in order that I may receive it back again. No one takes My life away from Me. I give it up of My own free will. I have the right to give it up, and I have the right to take it back. This is what My Father has commanded Me to do.
>
> JOHN 10:17-18

Tedium to Te Deum

These words spoken by Jesus have meaning for parents of a handicapped child. They know that even as Jesus was able to say, "The Father loves Me because I am willing to give up My life," so they can know and believe that this is true for them also. Christian parents of a handicapped child give up their lives willingly because the Holy Spirit has created in them the willingness to do so. He has given them the ability to discern God's gift of a spiritual life with Him.

As Christian parents you hear the truth of God's Word. The Holy Spirit living in you leads you to respond in the model of Christ. It is with a sense of dedication that you can say, "I am willing to give up my life, in order that I may receive it back again." Yes, Christian parents of a handicapped child prompted by God's Holy Spirit, give up this earthly life of their own free will. No one takes their life away from them. It is a voluntary choice to accept their handicapped child into their home if at all possible, and not have him placed in an institution.

But with their very commitment to Christ and His holy Word, God not only strengthens their commitment but also grants them a blessing. In rejecting their earthly life, such parents cut themselves free from the entanglements of the follies of humanity; the tinsel glitter of human ambition loses its luster. The beauty of life is found in its simplicity. Long hours of tedium are offset by an awareness of the spiritual joy of this simplicity. The incongruity of the handicapped child to the world in which he lives magnifies for the parents the incongruity of the handicapped child to the world in standards of the Truth. It is at such moments that the Comforter comes to parents of a handicapped child so that they willingly crucify the *i* of their existence and ted*i*um becomes their Te Deum, their "We Praise Thee, O God."

> "Even the hairs of your head have all been counted. So do not be afraid."
> LUKE 12:7

Be Not Afraid It Is I

"Why?, Why, Lord? Why me? Why me, O Lord?" is one question that no one can reason for himself. the words of our meditation tell us, "Do not be afraid." Why? Because God the Father, our God, is a personal God. His decrees are both universal and specific, both objective and subjective. Jesus tells us that God knows us individually down to the number of hairs on each person's head.

These very words, though, are often a dilemma for parents of a handicapped child. "If God really loved us," such parents often ask, "if God really loved us and created our bodies knowing the number of hairs on each person's head, why did He allow us to have a handicapped infant?"

It is perfectly natural that this unsolvable question, "Why?" should lurk in our hearts. But, like a coiling serpent, this question marks the presence of the Evil One, who would lead us to despair.

Like our first parents, we parents of a handicapped child are tempted to doubt by Satan himself. He poses the question, "Did God really tell you . . .?" in a thousand different ways. Thus Satan makes sinners of us all.

No one here on earth today can really answer the question, "Why?" In the case of the man born blind Jesus said it happened "so that God's power might be seen at work in him." Job never really received an answer when he asked why God allowed so much affliction to come to him. God simply pointed to His own wisdom, saying in effect that He knew what He was doing.

God points us away from the question "Why?" and points us toward His great love for us, as shown by Christ's death on the cross. He also points us toward our child and encourages us to love that child with a love that is at least somewhat like His love.

With the abiding love of their heavenly Father in their hearts, parents can forget about the "Why?" and concentrate on lovingly helping their child.

Christ is like a single body,
which has many parts;
it is still one body, even though
it is made up of different parts.
In the same way all of us,
Jews and Gentiles,
whether slaves or free,
have been baptized
into the one body
by the same Spirit,
and we have all been given
the one Spirit to drink.
For the body itself is not made
up of only one part,
but of many parts.
If the foot were to say,
"Because I am not a hand,
I don't belong to the body,"
that would not keep it
from being a part of the body.
And if the ear were to say,
"Because I am not an eye,
I don't belong to the body,"
that would not keep it
from being a part of the body.
If the whole body were just an eye,
how could it hear?
And if it were only an ear,
how could it smell?
As it is, however,
God put every different part
in the body
just as He wanted it to be.
There would not be a body
if it were all only one part!
As it is, there are many parts
but one body.

So then,
the eye cannot say to the hand,
"I don't need you!"
Nor can the head say to the feet,
"Well, I don't need you!"
On the contrary, we cannot do
without the parts of the body
that seem to be weaker;
and those parts that we think
aren't worth very much
are the ones which we treat
with greater care;
while the parts of the body
which don't look very nice
are treated with special modesty,
which the more beautiful parts
do not need.
God himself has put the body
together in such a way
as to give greater honor to
those parts that need it.
And so,
there is no division in the body,
but all its different parts
have the same concern
for one another.
If one part of the body suffers,
all the other parts
suffer with it;
if one is praised,
all the other parts
share its happiness.
All of you
are Christ's body,
and each one
is a part of it.

1 CORINTHIANS 12:12-27

The Sum of the Parts

How applicable the words of our text are to the plight of handicapped persons and their families. Whereas the pride of human natures causes some people to reject the handicapped as being unneeded, God regards them with the same love He has for all people everywhere. Handicapped Christians are part of the body of Christ and perform a necessary function there, although it may not be evident to the casual observer.

Parents in their special relationship with their handicapped children know the spiritual blessings they can receive through them. They know that their children are consecrated to be vessels of the Holy Spirit and that these children can often lead their parents to see the value of the one thing needful. They can help them to see the beam in their own eye—and also help them see Christ's love, which so often shines most brightly through the lives of the most helpless members of His body.

However, when even the least of Christ's children are rejected, His body suffers injury. It is as though Christ Himself were being hurt.

When he is rejected, the handicapped person lives with rejection; he grows with it; he endures it. Yet when cursed he does not answer back with a curse; when he suffers, he does not threaten. In his weakness the handicapped person stands uniquely alone—a model of the Suffering Servant.

> Jesus said,
> "My sheep listen to My voice;
> I know them,
> and they follow Me.
> I give to them eternal life,
> and they shall never die.
> No one can snatch them
> away from Me."
> JOHN 10:27-28

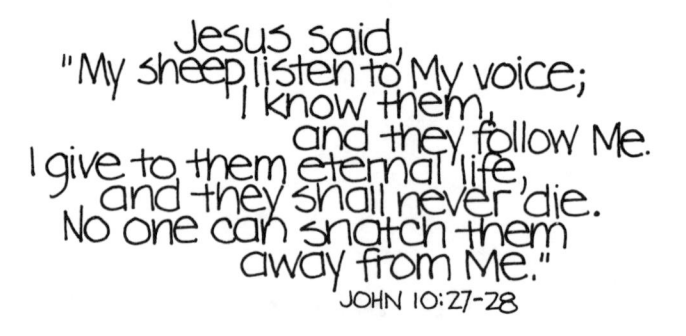

Recalled to Life

"Recalled to life." These famous words in Charles Dickens' historical novel *A Tale of Two Cities* refer to Dr. Manette, who was set free after years of imprisonment. "Recalled to life" are also words that refer to handicapped infants born of Christian parents. Recalled to life, not the life of this world but the life of a child of God. Recalled to life by Christian parents who have their infant children baptized in the name of our Triune God: Father, Son, and Holy Spirit. Recalled to life, the life of the Spirit living in the hearts of handicapped children, giving them hope, giving them peace in the assurance that their sins too, are forgiven.

"Recalled to life," yes, recalled to a life of service dedicated to the Lord of glory. Yes, a handicapped child as a child of God lives his new life as do all other children of God singing forth the praises of Him who made him or her. The union between God and the newborn person is a spiritual union. We express our joy in the individuality of the gifts God has given His children. The praises of the handicapped child are as pleasing to God as the praises of all other children of God, great and small.

With God all things are possible; therefore, with

God working through you, God's love comes to your child even as it does to all Christian children. You are not alone. You stand among all other parents who are dedicated to the will of God. Your child stands among all the lambs of Christ. Even as "man cannot live on bread alone, but needs every word that God speaks," so your child will live by the love of Christ which you give him.

There is a danger that parents of handicapped children face: They may not remain constant in giving their children the love and Christian nuture they need.

"Recalled to life," not only this life there on earth, but the life eternal with God in heaven, beginning now; for "He [Christ] will change our weak mortal bodies and make them like His own glorious body, using that power by which He is able to bring all things under His rule."

After receiving the news that Lazarus was ill unto death, Jesus waited two more days. Then on the third day Jesus went to His friends' home in Bethany. Why did He wait? Jesus replied, . . . so that you will believe." This is the challenge Christ gives to parents of handicapped children: . . . so that you will believe." God loves you, God loves you even in your seeming defeat. Even as Jesus called forth to Lazarus, "Come out!" so He calls forth to this handicapped infant, "Come out . . . come out to life." Not the life that the world beholds, but the new life of sonship with God the Father. To this life and to this hope the Spirit of Adoption calls both parents and child. In this oneness of faith and love both the parents and their gift from God live and have their being.

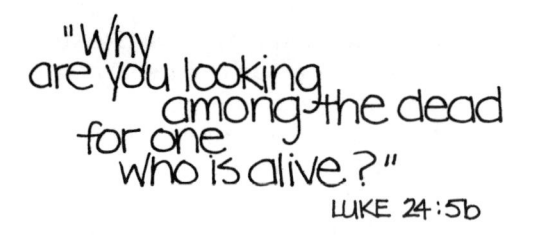

"Why are you looking among the dead for one who is alive?"

LUKE 24:5b

The Message of God's Hope

Repeatedly we hear the analogy that the grief which parents experience at the birth of their handicapped child is like the grief experienced at the death of a loved one. Therefore the words of the Easter angel, "Why are you looking among the dead for one who is alive?" must become God's message of hope for parents of a newborn handicapped infant. "Man looks at the outward appearance, but I look at the heart" God says. Against all outward appearances, against all human reason, against all human depression, the infant you hold in your arms is not dead, but lives. The Bible tells us that the servants called out to the nobleman of Capernaum, "Thy son liveth!" *(KJV)*. As the Easter angel declares to the family of a handicapped child, "He is risen," they return the greating, "He is risen indeed!"

The assurance that Christ died and rose for all, including handicapped infants, gives parents the spiritual fortitude to carry on. We recall Christ's words to Thomas "Blessed are they that have not seen and yet have believed" *(KJV);* for Christ gives such parents the challenge to believe and keep on believing that Christ loves them and that their infant will also be a joy and a blessing for them and their entire family as he grows up gaining favor with God and man.

The handicapped child is living testimony that all life—even though imperfect by the world's standards—is sacred. Life—all of it—is God's gift to His creatures to enjoy. It is God's gift to show forth His glory. When God gave us the gift of His Son, who rose on Easter monring, He gave us an Easter joy that gives us parents the true joy of salvation. "Don't be afraid . . . it is I!"

> Yet now hear,
> O Jacob My servant;
> and Israel,
> whom I have chosen:
> Thus saith the Lord
> that made thee,
> and formed thee from the womb,
> which will help thee;
> fear not,
> O Jacob My servant.
>
> ISAIAH 44:1-2 KJV

No Idle Coincidence

This Messianic passage has a fitting application in our lives. God speaks: "Yet now hear, O Jacob My servant." "Now"—the present is important; when God speaks, it is with urgency; it cannot be put off until later. God calls attention to the importance of His message with the admonition for the hearer to listen intently.

God begins with an address of respect: "O," for God created His creature man a little lower than the angels; God respects His creatures. God calls His people "Jacob My servant." As God called the patriarch Jacob by the name which means "he who grasps the heel," we are reminded not only of God's original promise to Eve, but also of the twin births of Jacob and Esau, and of Jacob's wrestling with the Lord at Peniel. God, in extending the hope of a Savior to Adam and Eve, also holds out this same hope to us. As Jacob wrestled with the Lord at Peniel, so we wrestle with this same Lord and come from our battle with a new name too: Israel, "he who wrestles with God."

In God's new covenant relationship with us

parents, He declares: "You shall be My people, and I will be your God" *(RSV)*. In this relationship we parents learn to persevere with God, for God has given us the victory through our Lord Jesus Christ. Jacob is the Lord's servant; he is possessed (owned) by God. Israel was chosen by God to be His spiritual son. It was no idle coincidence that God chose Israel, and it is no idle coincidence that God chooses the parents of a handicapped child for this servant role. When the Lord created Jacob there was no question as to who made him, and when the Lord made the parents of a handicapped child, there was no question who made them. Similarly, there can be no question as to who made the handicapped child himself. The Lord who formed Jacob in the womb also formed the handicapped child in the womb, making him a personal creature of God, respected by God.

Even as the Lord who made Jacob helped him, so He who made the handicapped child will help him. In this wrestling with God, Jacob is reborn Israel; in their wrestling with God about their problems, the parents are taught to persevere with Him. The Lord recognizes the magnitude of their trial, and so He whispers His message of peace:

"Fear not, O Jacob My servant." Spiritual wrestling will bring spiritual change. He will give the family the necessary strength to bear the burden. It is in this service to the Lord that parents and other members of the family of a handicapped child are His and He is theirs.

> Much is required from the person to whom much is given; much more is required from the person to whom much more is given.
>
> LUKE 12:48b

Hidden Resources

This passage of Scripture is a light that lights the way for us parents. It creates peace and acceptance in the hearts of us children of God. On the one hand, it teaches us that our gifts and resources come from Him. They are God's personal gift to each one of us as He chooses to give them. Therefore no one is in a position to boast about his resources, or skills; they are not something for which he is responsible. Since no one can claim credit for these gifts, a Christian is grateful to God for them, whether he has many or few. Christian parents can even thank God for their gifts—though they may be few—which He has given to their handicapped child.

God gives us our gifts and resources so that, motivated by thanksgiving and awe, we may be the means through which His grace is expressed. God gives His gifts to each person as it pleases Him. The person to whom God has given much is the agent through which many expressions of His grace can occur. The person to whom God has given more can demonstrate the same grace of God even more abundantly. In the case of parents of a handicapped child, God does not demand more from them than what He has given to them. Therefore no trial will be too great to carry. God demands only according to the gifts He has given each parent personally. The more a parent or other member of the family has been given, the more God demands of that person. The resources that enable members of the family to cope with a handicapped child have been placed within them by a gracious and loving God.

Love is patient;
love is kind and envies no one.
Love is never boastful,
nor conceited,
nor rude;
never selfish,
not quick to take offense.
Love keeps no score of wrongs;
does not gloat
over other men's sins,
but delights in the truth.
There is nothing
love cannot face;
there is no limit to its faith,
its hope,
and its endurance.
Love will never
come to an end.
I CORINTHIANS 13:4-8 NEB

Love That Endures

As Pilate asked Jesus, "What is truth?" the world needs to ask, "What is love?" the love that transcends all understanding. St. Paul begins the definition by saying: "Love is patient." In this patient love, parents learn to be patient with the child God has given them.

"Love is kind," and in the kindness of the parents their handicapped child learns to be kind. It is this kindness of the Son that the child reflects to others.

"Love . . . envies no one." In accepting the will of God, we Christian parents radiate this acceptance to the child. And the child learns to be "giving." Love does not envy, and we parents of a special child treasure our child as the gift of God that he is. We ponder God's wisdom with men, as Mary, the mother of Jesus, pondered and kept all these things in her heart; but, with God's help, we do not envy any other parents the child God has given to them. The handicapped child is God's perfect gift to us—perfect in the love of Christ who died and lives for our child too.

The simple words of St. Paul simply stated cry out in truth. Out of love come faith, hope and endurance. Endurance. That's what we will need. And we can get it through the Christian love that comes from faith in Christ our Savior.

When I was a child,
my speech, my outlook,
and my thoughts
were all childish.
When I grew up,
I had finished with childish things.
Now we see only
puzzling reflections in a mirror,
but then we shall see
face to face.
My knowledge is now partial;
then it will be whole,
like God's knowledge of me.
In a word,
there are three things
that last forever:
faith, hope, and love;
but the greatest
of them all
is love.

1 CORINTHIANS 13: 11-13 NEB

Face to Face

St. Paul uses the comparison of a child's developmental growth to help his Corinthian believers better understand their spiritual growth. He says a child's speech, outlook, and thoughts are childish. To be childish is to be self-centered, to be interested primarily in one's self, one's own pleasures, one's own desires, and one's own happiness at the expense of others. The apostles points to his own speech, his own outlook, his own thoughts. He examines his own self.

Parents of a handicapped child can learn from St. Paul's example. They can examine themselves; they can examine their own childish speech, their childish outlook, and their childish thoughts. They can remember foolish words formed by their tongues. "When I grew up," St. Paul says, "I had finished with childish things." So the parents of a handicapped child finish with childish spiritual concerns. Eventually they must choose between childish concerns and the one thing needful. As the disciples who followed Jesus before His death did not know His purpose fully, so parents do not always understand God's purposes; they see only puzzling reflections in the mirror of daily living; they do not always know themselves, their own hearts. The reflections they see call out to them to know themselves spiritually. Their guide through these puzzling reflections is Jesus the Good Shepherd. He leads them to that future time when they shall see God face to face. Like Moses and Jesus' disciples on the mount, they shall behold God's glory. They shall stand in God's presence.

Then their knowledge will be complete; they will know God as He knows them now. This intimate relationship will last forever. In this knowledge Christian parents will experience the enlightening work of the Holy Spirit, the hope of the resurrection in Christ, and the love of God. In His love they and all other Christians shall have everlasting union with Christ.

> Get rid of all bitterness,
> passion and anger.
> No more shouting or insults,
> no more hateful feelings
> of any sort!
> Instead,
> be kind and tender-hearted
> to one another
> and forgive one another,
> as God has forgiven you
> through Christ.
> Since you are God's dear children,
> you must try to be like Him.
> Your life
> must be controlled by love,
> just as Christ loved us
> and gave his life for us
> as a sweet-smelling offering
> and sacrifice
> that pleases God.
>
> EPHESIANS 4:31–5:2

A Life Controlled by Love

It is natural for parents who experience the birth of a handicapped child to also experience the subsequent whiplash that leads to bitterness, passion, and anger. In their slough of despondency, parents are tempted to become bitter, not only toward one another, but also subconsciously toward God. During the months preceding their child's birth, their anticipations were filled with hope for a child with gifts different from those with which God in His wisdom endowed him. In their bitterness, parents react with anger. It is an anger that smolders in their hearts and then breaks forth in shoutings and insults to the people around them.

It is at this point that St. Paul calls us back to reestablish the foundation of our personality in Christ: "No more hateful feelings of any sort!" Feelings come from the heart, and hate and love cannot live together there. So St. Paul changes our direction: "Instead, be kind and tender-hearted to one another." "Tender-hearted"—what a beautiful word in its Christian meaning! Parents of a handicapped child can be kind to their child, but to be tender-hearted encompasses a much more intimate relationship of oneness and understanding. To be tender-hearted is to have a warmness, a sensitivity, a soft place in one's heart that finds expression in the parents' living in forgiveness with each other, not in a superficial manner but as deeply as God has forgiven them in Christ. God's forgiveness took place in the past, so such parents do not dwell on the past in their lives but move forward as they follow Jesus the Good Shepherd. As dear children of God, they look to the life of Christ and follow His example of love and forgiveness. With Christ they say: "Forgive them Father! They don't know what they are doing."

The lives of Christian parents are controlled by the love of Christ. It is a love that remembers how Christ gave His life so that they might live also. With Christ as their example, such parents can then willingly give their own lives as a sweet-smelling offering of appreciation to the God who loved them. Then acts of devotion are a sacrifice brought, not in order to merit a reward, but out of love for Christ, who gave Himself as a sacrifice for all people.

What I mean, brothers, is that what is made of flesh and blood cannot share in God's kingdom, and what is mortal cannot possess immortality. Listen to this secret truth: we shall not all die, but when the last trumpet sounds, we shall all be changed in an instant, as quickly as the blinking of an eye. For when the trumpet sounds, the dead will be raised, never to die again, and we shall all be changed. For what is mortal must be changed into what is immortal; what will die must be changed into what cannot die. So when this takes place, and the mortal has been changed into the immortal, then the scripture will come true:
"Death is destroyed; victory is complete!"
"Where, Death, is your power to hurt?"
Death gets its power to hurt from sin, and sin gets its power from the Law.

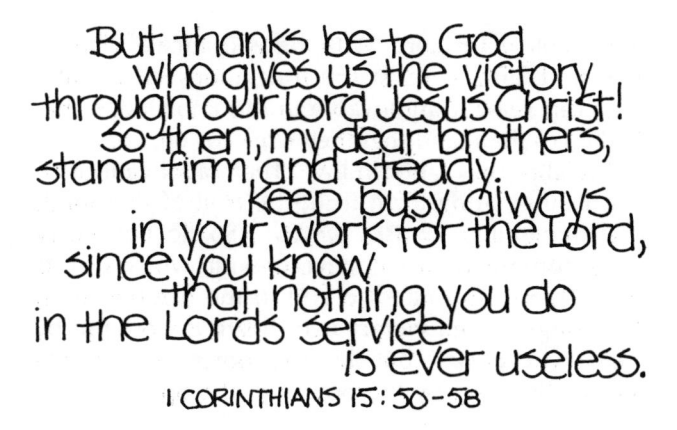

> But thanks be to God who gives us the victory through our Lord Jesus Christ! So then, my dear brothers, stand firm and steady. Keep busy always in your work for the Lord, since you know that nothing you do in the Lord's service is ever useless.
>
> I CORINTHIANS 15:50-58

Service That Never Loses Its Value

These words of St. Paul to the Corinthians speak also to the family of a handicapped child. Here is the hope that lies in the hearts of all Christians everywhere. We can look beyond this world to the next, when we and all believers in Christ shall be changed. Then the weak, perishable body shall be clothed with the imperishable spiritual body. The "eternity" of time that parents of a handicapped child see in their situation in this world loses its power. Gone is the frustration of aloneness; gone is the frustration of the immediacy of the problem; gone is the frustration of a frantic search for help for their child; for at the end of life there is victory. The perishable being will become immortal. Then death works a new beginning, a new beginning in our Lord Jesus Christ, a new beginning with a new body. This body shall be immortal. This beginning shall have no end.

It is the joy of this victory that gives Christian parents the spiritual strength to stand firm and immovable in the Lord. With the assurance of victory, they find faith to resist the frustrations of this life. They can remain immovable in the knowledge that God loves them and that they work for the Lord, and in this labor they labor in love. Their labor cannot be lost. It must bring forth fruit, the fruit of the Spirit. They remember Christ's words: "So do not worry about tomorrow; it will have enough worries of its own. There is no need to add to the troubles each day brings." Their victory over death is won, not by their own power but by the power of Christ's resurrection and by the power of the Spirit.

> I am telling you the truth:
> a grain of wheat remains no more
> than a single grain
> unless it is dropped
> into the ground and dies.
> If it does die,
> then it produces
> many grains.
> Whoever loves his own life
> will lose it;
> whoever hates his own life
> in this world
> will keep it for life eternal.
> Whoever wants to serve Me
> must follow Me,
> so that My servant
> will be with Me
> where I am.
> And My Father
> will honor
> him who serves Me.
>
> JOHN 12:24-26

Many from One

By means of a grain of wheat Jesus explains the nature of a life dedicated to God. If a grain of wheat remains intact, it remains a single grain of wheat. But when it is dropped into the ground and dies, it produces many grains. Similarly, parents of a handicapped child who attempt to keep their life for themselves will save that life for their own interest or pleasure. But when they take on Christ and, so to speak, give up this earthly life by serving their handicapped child, then they will keep their life for life eternal.

Parents of a "special" child, like all Christian parents everywhere, portray the lives of our first parents, that first Adam, that first Eve. Even as the promise of the Savior was fulfilled through the first Adam and Eve, whereby many people who followed them came to the knowledge of truth and were saved, so the fruits of faith and discipleship of Christian parents of a handicapped child bear witness to the truth that God is Love. Jesus' remark, "Whoever loves his own life will lose it; whoever hates his own life in this world will keep it for life eternal," is echoed by St. Paul. In his Letter to the Romans he writes: "We who have the Spirit as the first of God's gifts also groan within ourselves as we wait for God to make us His sons and set our whole being free."

Even as the single grian of wheat produces the full ear, so the Christian parent of a handicapped child wants to serve Christ by following Him. Such a parent wants to follow Christ's example of service and sacrifice. The Christian's reward for this life of service and sacrifice in faith is not a substitute for Christ's suffering and death, but rather a natural outgrowth of that faith in Christ. Helping their child to grow in the grace of God is a service that parents perform for Christ.

Jesus says "My servant," for we indeed are owned by Him, having been purchased with His blood. As servants of Christ we carry out God's will: the will of Him who sent Christ into the world. Christian parents of a handicapped child have the confidence that they, too, will be with Christ in heaven. And with this promise God the Father, our Creator, honors such parents even as He honors all followers of Christ.

> The man who goes
> in through the gate
> is the shepherd of the sheep.
> The gatekeeper opens
> the gate for him;
> the sheep hear his voice
> as he calls his own sheep
> by name,
> and he leads them out.
> When he has brought them out,
> he goes ahead of them,
> and the sheep follow him,
> because they know his voice.
> They will not follow someone else;
> instead, they will run away
> from such a person,
> because they do not know
> his voice.
>
> JOHN 10:2-5

Moving with Hope

The man who goes in by the door is the shepherd of the sheep. Jesus is the Good Shepherd. Jesus is that man, the Son of Man. Jesus knows our needs; He knows our desires. Jesus suffered as a man; He suffered as we do. The help He offers is offered with the knowledge of what it means to suffer as parents of a handicapped child may suffer.

When the sheep hear the shepherd's voice, they know it is their shepherd. When we hear the voice of Jesus, we know it is our Shepherd. We know His voice because it is the voice of love and compassion. As the shepherd calls his sheep, Jesus calls us by the Gospel. His message of God's love fills us with confidence. We can move with hope, following the

Good Shepherd who goes ahead of us. Jesus calls us by name; He knows us personally; He knows us individually; therefore He knows our needs, He knows our sorrows. The sheep follow Him out to green pastures. Jesus provides for our needs, He sustains us with the bread of life; He gives His body and blood.

So Jesus leads us out of our dilemma. Jesus knows the way ahead; He is the Good Shepherd; He sees beyond our valley of the shadow of death, the valley of despair, the valley of unbelief. We follow Him because we know His voice. His Word is truth. We know the voice of God as Moses did when he stood before the burning bush and heard the thunder of the great I Am, as Elijah did when he heard the soft whisper of the wind and knew that it was God who spoke to him. "Don't be afraid," Jesus called out to His disciples, and down through the centuries His followers, His disciples, His friends, the Shepherd's sheep, have heard His voice. When we hear that voice, we are not afraid, for He is with us. His rod and His staff are the signs of His authority and power; they are the signs of His love and protection. In the same manner the handicapped child is a visible sign of god's presence, of His love, of His continuing protection. The world, our sinful flesh, and the devil would have us deny these signs and forsake the Good Shepherd. But as the small child finds peace and reassurance in hearing the voice of his parents, so parents of a handicapped child find the spiritual peace that goes beyond all understanding when they hear the voice and the message of love and forgiveness that Jesus breathes out to them.

We remain firm in the faith to which Jesus calls us. We hear the voice of temptation; it is real. Parents of a handicapped child are tempted to give up; they are tempted to say, "It's too much," but they recognize that evil voice for what it is—the temptation to put down their cross, to climb out of their valley of despair without the help of the Good Shepherd. But they resist this temptation; they run away from it; their ears listen intently for the voice of their own true Shepherd. To follow the Good Shepherd is to live in freedom. To follow the Evil One is to give up this freedom and live the life of a slave enmeshed in self-pity and despair.

Christian parents of a handicapped child follow Jesus. Even as Jesus denied the desires of His flesh and took up His cross willingly, so such parents take up their cross by the power of the Holy Spirit, the Comforter. By His power, through the Word, such Christian parents live their lives in faith.

> "How can a grown man be born again?" Nicodemus asked. "He certainly cannot enter his mother's womb and be born a second time!" "I am telling you the truth," replied Jesus, "that no one can enter the Kindom of God unless he is born of water and the Spirit. A person is born physically of human parents, but he is born spiritually of the Spirit. Do not be surprised because I tell you that you must all be born again."
> JOHN 3:4-7

To Be Born Again

To be born again! At the birth of a handicapped child, time stands still and the parents' thoughts race backward, searching for some clue, some way to find causes, a way to explain their predicament, to pinpoint some specific evidence that says, "If only this would not have happened, if only we would not have done that, etc., if only we had the opportunity to relive the past in order to prevent the handicapping of our newborn infant!"

To be born again! Reason, intellect would have parents wish for that opportunity even as Nicodemus questioned the Lord's statement: "To be born again? How? A grown man?" The family of a handicapped child stands perplexed even as Nicodemus did—man grown old with the cares of this life, grown cold with lack of faith and trust in the gracious good will of a loving God. Jesus tells it as it is: "You must be born again."

But parents and other members of the family are tempted to cling to their reason. A grown man should put off the cares of this life and be born again? But Jesus speaks the truth to Nicodemus as He did to Pontius Pilate, as He does to a distressed family. Just as Pilate was troubled when he heard Jesus' words, so parents, brothers and sisters, grandparents are troubled. "What does this mean?" they ask. Despair, doubt, unbelief drive them to question the personal love of God for them and their child.

"Born of water and the Spirit!" As ordinary, everyday water is the visible sign of God's promise of salvation; as Jesus the man, in all His rejection and weakness, is the visible sign of God with us, Immanuel—so the handicapped child is the visible sign of God's love for us. Our own flesh leads us to seek answers that relate to this world, to our earthly lives. But Jesus would have us take courage in the Spirit, in the hope we have in Christ, in the hope that is ours through Baptism, the Word of promise made visible in the water.

To be born again! As we have been born again through the water and the Word in Baptism, so our handicapped child lives under that same grace. What we cannot do, God through Christ can. When Jesus says, "Let the children come to Me," His invitation goes out to all children, including those who are handicapped. In His love all the members of the family can live and have their being, not only their physical being, but also and more important their spiritual being. In this love both parents and child grow in their knowledge of the wisdom that surpasses all human understanding. As parents witness this spiritual understanding in their handicapped child, they find peace and the assurance that Christ lives in their child too.

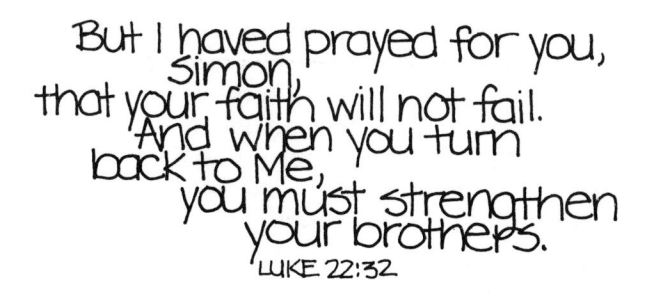

> But I haved prayed for you, Simon,
> that your faith will not fail.
> And when you turn back to Me,
> you must strengthen your brothers.
> LUKE 22:32

Strengthened Through Prayer

In these words Jesus is personally involved, personally concerned with Simon. Jesus says, "I have prayed." Jesus already knows Simon's needs; He speak to Simon, calls him by name. Jesus is our personal Savior too, our personal Redeemer and Lord.

"Teach us to pray," the disciples had asked Jesus; so He did. Then Jesus used this same power to keep Peter in the faith. Jesus pleads with the Spirit, the Comforter. Jesus is our Advocate with the Father also. He prays for the parents of a handicapped child. He speaks to the Father, the Creator. He speaks to the Holy Spirit: "Send forth Your light, O Holy Spirit, that these parents may know Your name aright. Send forth Your power, Your strength, that they may not lose sight of God's love for them and for their child."

"Teach us to pray," the disciples asked. Christian parents of a special child walk in that same way, learning to pray, learning to talk with God, learning to search out His wisdom, His power, His strength. Even as Jesus went away alone to pray, so such parents in their solitude find the comfort of God's Spirit in prayer.

Jesus saw ahead to the future; He knew that

Peter would turn back to Him, not because of Peter's strength, not because of his power, but because of Jesus' power, because of Jesus' foresight to pray God to help Peter to resist the temptation that was to come, the temptation to despair. And Peter did turn back; he was turned around. Peter had stood face to face with Christ on the mount and had said, "Lord, how good it is that we are here!" And it was good that he had been there, for the radiance of Christ's power eventually filled Peter's heart.

So Jesus stands ready to pray for parents of a handicapped child to stay their faith against the onslaught of despair. Jesus is their Advocate too. Jesus looks ahead to the future and sees that these parents, too, will come to the knowledge of the truth and confess, "Lord, how good it is that we are here!" Standing in the radiance of Christ's glory, standing face to face, parents reflect the glory of God. God's love is reflected in their eyes; God's love is reflected in their joy. The smile that their handicapped child smiles reflects their own joy in Christ.

Jesus commands Peter, "When you turn back to Me, you must strengthen your brothers." It is a command of love; it is a command of joy-filled gratitude for what the Savior did for Peter. "Must" reveals duty, not an optional act, but it is a duty willingly chosen; it reveals obedience to God's will in gratitude and in response to His love.

So it is with Christian parents of a handicapped child. They have the opportunity to strengthen other parents of handicapped children. They have experienced the trials such parents face. They know the sustaining power of faith. They can say with assurance, "Come and see; come to the crib and see the child; wait and you shall see the Holy Child; wait and you shall behold His glory, the glory of the only begotten Son of God. Christ calls Christian parents of a handicapped child to strengthen one another; to strengthen other members of the family, such as grandparents; to strengthen other members of the household of faith, who may be carrying their own heavy burdens. If you will do this, then you are My disciples *in deed.*

Jesus looked at them and asked, "What then, does this scripture mean? 'The stone which the builders rejected as worthless turned out to be the most important of all.' Everyone who falls on that stone will be cut to pieces; and if the stone falls on someone, it will crush him to dust."

LUKE 20:17-18

Rejected Stones

Parents of a handicapped child see in these words of Scripture, not only a prototype of their Lord and Savior, the chosen one of Israel, but also a prototype of their child. Rejected by people who do not understand, who do not appreciate him, the handicapped child is nevertheless accepted by his parents.

St. Luke reports that Jesus the Savior, the Anointed One, the Messiah, looked at the people. His look was one of perceiving, of looking with depth, of knowing their inmost thoughts, of seeing the condition of their hearts. With His look Jesus also directed a question to them. It is a question to raise their spiritual sights; it is not a question to doubt the truth, but to believe it, to accept it. For this reason Jesus went to the Scriptures, God's Word, the Word God impelled holy men of God to record for all mankind to read, accept, and cherish in their hearts.

The stone of which Christ speaks is Christ Himself. Christ testified of Himself. Christ testified of the Father, and the Father testified of Him. "The Scriptures ... speak about Me!" Jesus exclaimed. The builders are the church leaders, those people who claimed to be the most important children of the Almgihty.

In rejecting Christ, those church leaders turned away from God. They did not recognize the value of Christ, the Son of God, and the value of His message of salvation. They created their own way; they had designed their own worship, their own political Messiah. In their blindness those who rejected the stone did not realize that the stone they rejected is the most important stone of any building of faith— the keystone, the stone on which the whole doorway rests, the stone through which or under which all who desire eternal life must travel.

The handicapped child raises Jesus' question, "What, then, does this scripture mean?" Christian families of a handicapped child see beyond their child to the risen Lord, their Savior and Friend. Such families look beyond their earthly experiences and accept their cross in the light of God's Word. Though the world may reject their child, they accept him and he becomes a precious part of their lives, a most important possession.

Though the world regards the gift of intelligence as the most important characteristic of human life, the families of the handicapped learn that God's greatest gift to mankind is the gift of love. They come to know that a handicapped child has this gift of love to offer. Reject such a gift? Never! Rather welcome this special child with its special gift of love—a love that reminds us of the Giver of every good and perfect gift, the Giver of life and salvation.

> He said to another man,
> "Follow Me."
> But that man said,
> "Sir, first let me go back
> and bury my father."
> Jesus answered,
> "Let the dead
> bury their own dead.
> You go and proclaim
> the kingdom of God."
> Another man said,
> "I will follow you, sir;
> but first let me go
> and say good-bye to my family."
> Jesus said to him,
> "Anyone who starts to plow
> and then keeps looking back
> is of no use
> for the Kingdom of God."
> LUKE 9:59-62

First Let Me Go

When Jesus invited a man, "Follow Me," He urged him to take up his cross, to accept the challenges of faith. But the man's reply was an indirect refusal to do so. When the man addressed Jesus with the word "Sir," he showed respect for Jesus as a teacher, one having a following, one having a message of importance. But when the man asked, "First let me go back and bury my father," he revealed his priorities in life. He wanted to be excused temporarily. He saw the value of Christ as the Messiah, but in effect he told Jesus that he had something more important to do. He wanted the freedom to be concerned with earthly things first.

Jesus did not accept the man's excuse, for He recognized the rejection in the man's heart.

They that are likeminded will gather together. The spiritually dead will appeal to those who are spiritually dead, but those who live by the Spirit seek out others who live by the Spirit. In Jesus's answer to the man, He warned him of the danger of being a spiritual son of his dead father. What advice does Jesus give this man? Jesus says, "You go and proclaim the Kingdom of God." Jesus directs His answer personally to the man, "You"; Jesus is concerned personally with this man's spiritual state. "Go," Jesus says. The man should extol the Kingdom of God; he should invite others to come into the Kingdom of God.

So Jesus invites parents and all others who care for handicapped children to center their lives in the Kingdom of God. "Go and proclaim," Jesus tells parents. Invite others to come into the Kingdom—by your example of faith, by believing in and seeing the love of God for all mankind beyond the outward condition of your child, by knowing and believing that your child is among the spiritual children of God's family and that someday he or she too will share the joys of heaven wearing a spiritually perfect body. The handicapped child stands as the visible reminder that all believers are in need of the renewal that is coming when God's children will rise wearing their spiritual, perfect bodies. In effect, the handicapped child preaches the Kingdom of God by his very presence.

When the second man approached Jesus with the same kind of excuse, "First let me go and say good-bye to my family," we are reminded of Jesus' words to His own family. When Jesus' relatives could not understand His message of the promised Messiah and accept Him as the Son of God, He answered them: "Who is My mother? Who are My brothers? . . . Whoever does what My Father in heaven wants him to do is My brother, My sister, and My mother." The Spiritual bonds of God's family surpass the bonds that unite brothers and sisters of the flesh. So it is with the handicapped child; it is of secondary importance that the handicapped child is seed and flesh of the parents. Above all, he or she is a child of God; it is this spiritual union between the child and the parent that creates the only true, the only lasting bond between them. Parents, grandparents, pastors, and teachers of a handicapped child have the wonderful opportunity not only to bring up the child physically but, more important, to nurture the child spiritually so that they can all be one through Christ, the Giver of every good and perfect gift.

> As Jesus was walking along,
> He saw a man
> who had been born blind.
> His disciples asked Him,
> "Teacher, whose sin
> caused him to be born blind?
> Was it his own,
> or his parents' sin?"
> Jesus answered,
> "His blindness has nothing to do
> with his sins
> or his parents' sins.
> He is blind so that God's power
> might be seen at work in him.
> As long as it is day,
> we must do the work
> of Him who sent Me;
> night is coming
> when no one can work.
> While I am in the world,
> I am the light for the world."
> —JOHN 9:1-5

So That God's Power May Be Seen

As Jesus walked along in the lives of His disciples, so also today He walks along in the lives of His people, leading us in our pilgrimage to come in contact with handicapped persons. And we, too, like the disciples of old, raise the same question in our hearts: "Who sinned? This person or his parents? Why, Lord? What did we do to deserve a handicapped child?" At these moments of doubt we question God's love; we retrench our spiritual beings. At these moments the devil holds up the law of God before us. At these moments he would condemn us before God; he would rob us of the free grace we have in Jesus our Lord and Savior. At these moments the devil would have us on our knees, but not to seek out the Holy Comforter, not to follow the example of Christ, who pleaded, "Father, if You will, take this cup of suffering away from Me. Not My will, however, but Your will be done."

But thanks be to God and our Lord Jesus Christ. He answers the devil for us. A person's handicap has nothing to do with sin, neither his sin, nor his parents' sins. What is important is that through this man's handicap God's power might be seen at work in his life. God's power at work in him—the power that changes blindness into sight, lameness into wholeness, the power that creates faith to believe God's wonderful promises of His grace of forgiveness. As Christ changed the man's blindness into the perfection of sight, so God changes our spiritual beings into perfection through the death of His only begotten Son. The curing of the man's physical infirmity is the visible sign of God's power to create faith, to forgive sins, to announce salvation to sinners.

As Christ continued to do the works of Him who sent Him, so Christian parents and teachers of a handicapped child continue to nurture the child in the same love that God has bestowed on them. Not for an hour, not for a day, but for as long as they are needed by the handicapped child and are in a position to help, they stand in Christ's stead. They are the light of the world to the child. As they shine, so the child reflects that light of Christ back to them.

> And He said to them all,
> "If anyone wants to come with Me,
> he must forget himself,
> take up his cross every day,
> and follow Me.
> For whoever wants to save his own life will lose it,
> but whoever loses his life for My sake will save it.
> Will a person gain anything if he wins the whole world
> but is himself lost or defeated?
> Of course not!
> If a person is ashamed of Me and of My teaching,
> then the Son of Man will be ashamed of him
> when He comes in His glory
> and in the glory of the Father
> and of the holy angels.
>
> LUKE 9:23-26

An Invitation to Love

Jesus here extends an invitation to all people everywhere; no one is excluded. But it is an invtiation. No one is forced to accept it. So too with the parents and teachers of a handicapped child. God invites them to take up their cross and follow Him. Jesus says, "If you want to; that is, if you have the desire to do so, then come with Me." Those who accept Christ's invitation and help the handicapped are not alone; Jesus the Good Shepherd is with them. In doing this, Jesus says, such a person "must forget himself," forget this earthly life, forget personal earthly goals.

"Take up your cross," Jesus says, not for a day or a month or a year, but every day. Jesus says, "Take it up; don't ignore it; don't deny it, but take it up each day." So the parents and entire family of a handicapped child accept their God-given responsibility to love that child, to accept him, to understand him as a child of God. As they take up their cross each day, they do so with the prayer: "Not what I want, but what You want."

Jesus leads the way! With hope and gratitude parents follow their Savior. They trust Jesus will guide them. Each day they ask His divine help, for the person who directs his thoughts and actions to gain only earthly, perishable goals will lose sight of the spiritual, heavenly goals that Christ offers. On the other hand, whoever turns away from earthly goals and incentives, not for his own but for Jesus' sake, will gain his spiritual life with Christ in heaven. Parents of a handicapped child are tempted to accept the thinking of people who offer them reasons to avoid their duty of love and lay aside the arduous task of nurturing their child. They should take to heart instead the question Christ addressed to all people: "Will a person gain anything if he wins the whole world but is himself lost or defeated?"

The handicapped child stands in a similar relationship to its parents as Christ does to all people. If a person is ashamed of Jesus and of His teaching, "then the Son of Man will be ashamed of him." We are reminded of Peter's denial of Jesus. In the same manner parents are tempted to deny their child before men. Parents of a handicapped child often fear people and the hurts they can inflict. But Christian parents are sustained by the spiritual joys that the Son of Man gives them, but which are not visible to the world.

In a certain sense, as the Son of Man was the

Seed of the woman promised to fallen humanity, so the handicapped child stands as the spiritual hope of the parents. They know that when Jesus comes in His glory, power, might, and love in His second coming, they and their handicapped child shall receive the glory of the Father, Creator, and Preserver. Christian parents of a special child see the fulfillment of the promise of the coming Savior, the Messiah. In caring for their child, they forget themselves as they wait for the redemption of their bodies, as do all followers of Christ.

> He answered John's messengers, "Go back and tell John what you have seen and heard: the blind can see, the lame can walk, those who suffer from dreaded skin diseases are made clean, the deaf can hear, the dead are raised to life, and the Good News is preached to the poor! How happy are those who have no doubts about Me!"
> LUKE 7:22-23

How Happy to Have No Doubts

John the Baptist has asked Jesus: "Are you he who is to come, or shall we look for another?" (*RSV*). So Jesus answers John's messengers: "Go back and tell . . . what you have seen and heard." Jesus calls upon these men to be personal witnesses. He does not ask them to believe what He says about Himself. He tells them to look and listen. In the same manner parents of a handicapped child are called upon to be personal witnesses to tell what they have seen and heard in their own lives as to how God's love has come to them through their child.

As Jesus performed His miracle of re-creating the perfect body in giving sight to the blind, hearing to the deaf, and life to the dead, so parents of a special child visualize by faith the perfection of body that is to be, not only their child's but also their own. They see in their child's physical imperfections a visible sign of their own spiritual imperfections. As Christ's miracles were the visible sign of His spiritual power to forgive sins, so these parents look forward to the replacement of their own and their child's imperfect body by that same power.

Jesus does not stop with the evidence of His miracles, but He goes on: "The Good News is preached to the poor." This is the end point, the climax of Jesus' coming to be our Brother. He preached the Good News of salvation, the forgiveness of sins for all people everywhere. By word and deed Jesus gave evidence of His Sonship with God the Father.

As the poor of this world are a symbol of the spiritual destitution of all men, so the handicapped child is a symbol of the physical destitution that all men carry with them. Even as Jesus says, "Blessed are the poor in spirit" (KJV), so the handicapped child is blessed among all men. When parents see their child's limitations, they should anticipate the life to come, when their child will be whole. How filled they can be with spiritual joy in knowing and believing in the transforming Savior! How happy are they who do not doubt, who do not succumb to temptation and fears as to God's will and rule, but firmly see Jesus ruling in their own lives as Savior, Messiah, Lord, and King.

Parents can see in their handicapped child the dead raised to life; God's child who is impaired shall be raised to perfect life. Even as Christ was lifted up to life through the cross, faith-filled parents are lifted up through their cross to life eternal. As the cataracts fall from the eyes of the blind, so the spiritual cataracts of saddened parents fall from their eyes and they behold the glory and the power of God in their handicapped child. The lame in the text are healed physically. They receive the power to run and skip and jump. Burdened parents are healed spiritually.

They believe and trust and hope in Jesus their Savior from sin, wherever He leads them.

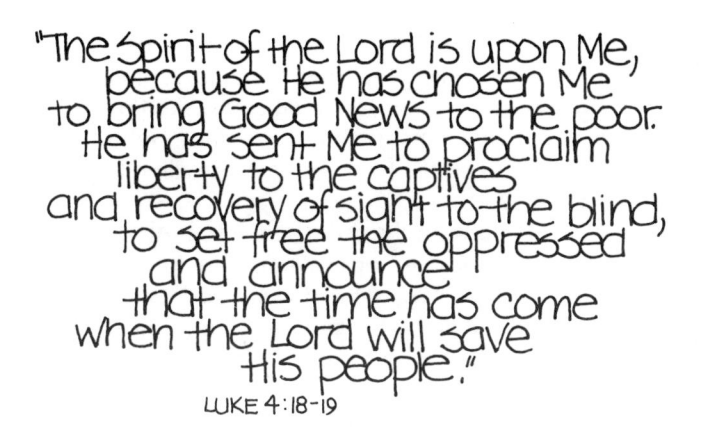

> "The Spirit of the Lord is upon Me, because He has chosen Me to bring Good News to the poor. He has sent Me to proclaim liberty to the captives and recovery of sight to the blind, to set free the oppressed and announce that the time has come when the Lord will save His people."
>
> LUKE 4:18-19

Prophet, Priest, and King

The figure of Christ the Suffering Servant becomes our figure also, for in His suffering our suffering becomes meaningful to us. As Christ the Savior-King was anointed by God "to bring Good News to the poor," so parents as God's children through Christ assume the role of prophet, priest, and king to one another. They speak of the hope that is theirs to live with Christ in His kingdom triumphant, they dedicate their lives as priests to offer their services of love, and they reign (now!) as kings in the family of God. Anointed with the Spirit through Baptism, such Christian parents proclaim the Good News to their own poor child. By their actions and words they proclaim the liberty all Christians have in Christ. In this liberty also their child can reach out beyond his handicapping condition and experience the joy of Christ's love.

Similarily, parents of a handicapped child recover their own spiritual sight; their eyes are opened and they behold the glory of the Father, the Son, and the Spirit. With this spiritual sight they see themselves as they are. They are a part of God's family; they no longer feel they are apart from God's love. In recovering their spiritual sight, such parents like all other believers in Christ are made righteous; the old Adam is put off every day; they live before God in their faith.

With His coming the Spirit sets free both parents and child from all oppression, including the callousness of so many who do not understand the child nor appreciate his longings to communicate the love that is locked within him. To both parents and child, and to all people everywhere, the Spirit announces the year when the Lord will save His people, all His people in Christ. The strong future tense "will save" leaves no doubt: All the Lord's people—including the handicapped child, his parents, his brothers and sisters, his grandparents—live in that state of grace.

> Your Father in heaven knows that you need all these things. Instead, be concerned above everything else with the Kingdom of God and with what He requires of you, and He will provide you with all these other things. So do not worry about tomorrow; it will have enough worries of its own. There is no need to add to the troubles each day brings.
>
> MATTHEW 6:32b-34

Provided with All Things

With these words of comfort Jesus directs parents of a handicapped child to His heavenly Father and theirs. As Father, God the Creator knows everything they need. His knowledge is universal; yet is is particular. God knows their needs intimately and intently. Therefore God the Holy Spirit would encourage them to look for and search out that one need which is most essential. Christ would have us, like Mary, choose the one thing needful: His Kingdom and that which God requires—a heart made clean in the blood of the Lamb. God follows with the promise that He will provide for everything else that the parents of a special child need. Their faith in the mercy of God puts their own lives into proper perspective. They can appreciate with thanksgiving Christ's statement: "Do not worry about tomorrow."

Parents live under the urgency to provide their child with all possible opportunities to grow and to develop to the greatest the potential that God his Creator gave him. When parents of a handicapped child bring him to God through Baptism, they can have the peace of knowing that they have chosen the one thing needful. In this blessed washing God makes their child His own and clothes him or her with the robe of His perfect righteousness. Such parents know that God will provide all other things that their child or they may need. They can meet each day with the confidence that both their child and they are in God's care.

Their concern for their child will be a lifelong concern, but for Christian parents this concern is grounded in the foundation of Jesus Christ. They know that their Father in heaven watches over them. His eternal view sees beyond their child's handicap, beyond their own frustration, and beyond the grave. God sees the child as he really is: a member of His family, His child, His son, His daughter. With the psalmist, Christian parents of a handicapped child can declare: "Leave all your worries with Him, because He cares for you."

> Be alert, be on watch!
> Your enemy, the Devil,
> roams around like a roaring lion,
> looking for someone to devour.
> Be firm in your faith
> and resist him,
> for you know
> that your fellow believers
> in all the world
> are going through
> the same kind of sufferings.
> But after you have suffered
> for a little while,
> the God of all grace,
> who calls you to share
> his eternal glory
> in union with Christ,
> will Himself perfect you
> and give you firmness, strength,
> and a sure foundation.
> To Him be the power forever!
> Amen.
>
> 1 PETER 5:8-11

The Glory That Is Going to Be

Peter tells his fellow believers to be alert, be on watch! Peter no doubt remembers his own denial of Christ vividly. That may be why he is so forceful. Like Christ's parable of the five wise virgins and the five foolish virgins that underscores the urgency of being vigilant for His second coming, Peter wants to make his friends feel the urgency of his alarm against the devil. The devil searches out his prey, his spiritual victims. He looks for anyone who is not on guard to resist his deceits.

When the cares of bringing up a handicapped child weigh heavily upon his parents, then the devil would like us to believe that we have no friends, that no one understands our problems, that no one sympathizes with our difficulties. In this state of forsakenness the devil comes to us parents with the temptation to deny the mercy of God. He tempts us to chafe under the physical and emotional strains of our daily living.

Peter advises his friends to be firm in their faith and resist the devil by using the power of the Word. Parents can look to Christ the Good Shepherd for this power. They can take comfort in Peter's words: "Your fellow believers in all the world are going through the same kind of sufferings." They are not alone in their trials; all other Christians experience the chastisement of God's love, too. It is with such sufferings that God keeps them in His peace. They remember St. Paul's words: "I consider that what we suffer at this present time cannot be compared at all with the glory that is going to be revealed to us." The suffering of parents of a handicapped child, like the suffering of all other Christians, is for a short time. God calls them to share His eternal glory in union with Christ. He is the Triune God: Creator, Redeemer, and Preserver. He is the God of all grace: that undeserved love which God offers to all people, including us. Peter states: "God . . . will perfect you." The Spirit gives us parents firmness in faith and spiritual strength in the sure foundation: Jesus Christ. We parents pray for this sustaining power of God.

> The servant does not deserve thanks for obeying orders, does he? It is the same with you; When you have done all you have been told to do, say, "We are ordinary servants; we have only done our duty."
> LUKE 17:9-10

As I Have Loved You

Jesus, the Great Teacher, uses this simple illustration from daily life to help His followers grow in spiritual understanding. The role of the servant becomes the role of all followers of Christ. When they have done all they have been told to do, they know they have only done their duty.

On the night Jesus was betrayed He prayed: "Take this cup of suffering from Me!" Parents of a handicapped child recognize this feeling; yet they realize that as the Father loved His Son Jesus, and yet did not remove the "cup of suffering," so Christ loves them. Beyond the temporary suffering, such Christian parents can expect and will discover the love that surpasses all understanding. It is spiritually reassuring to them to know that God's grace will be sufficient.

The Scriptures state: "Much is required from the person to whom much is given." But God also promises that the cross He gives us will never be more than we can bear. We do not attempt to fulfill God's demands by our own strength and effort; rather it is by His power that we serve to fulfill the new commandment that Christ, the Servant-King, gave us: "Love one another even as I have loved you."

Yes, those who serve the handicapped are ordinary servants, but ordinary servants of the Most High God. Believers in Christ have a dual relationship to life. They are not only humble servants, but they also hold within their hearts the joy of being the sons and daughters of the Most High God. Yes, they are princes and princesses—children of the Great King.

This gives a new, wonderful dimension to our difficult calling. It makes it easier to be patient and to extend love and compassion. The cross we parents of a handicapped child bear is monumental—not overwhelming, but monumental in the sense that it is a monument to Christ, the Cross-Bearer, and to His love for us. God promises to provide us with the spiritual resources to meet the challenge He has given us. Through Word and Sacrament, and also through the help of Christian friends and through the experiences of daily living, God builds that spiritual strength every day.

Christian parents of a handicapped child grow in their awareness that, though their cross may in fact be a heavy one, it is no greater than the resources God has given them to bear it. Such parents realize their relationship to all other children in God's family. So intimately does God know His people that He fits each person with the cross that person needs. So Christian parents come to realize and appreciate more fully the words of Jesus: "When you have done all you have been told to do, say, 'We are ordinary servants; we have only done our duty.'" Such parents may indeed be ordinary servants, but they are ordinary servants of the Most High God, and that makes all the differences.

We are no better
than pots of earthenware
to contain this treasure
[God's gift of faith],
and this proves
that such transcendent power
does not come from us,
but is God's alone.
Hard-pressed on every side,
we are never hemmed in;
bewildered,
we are never at our wits' end;
hunted, we are
never abandoned to our fate;
struck down,
we are not left to die.
Wherever we go
we carry death with us in our body
the death that Jesus died,
that in this body also
life may reveal itself,
the life that Jesus lives.
For continually, while still alive,
we are being surrendered
into the hands of death,
for Jesus' sake,
so that the life of Jesus
also may be revealed
in this mortal body of ours.
Thus death is at work in us,
and life in you.
But the Scripure says," I believed,
and therefore I spoke out,"
and we too,
in the same spirit of faith,
believe and therefore speak out
for we know that

He who raised
 the Lord Jesus to life
will with Jesus raise us too,
 and bring us to His presence,
  and you with us.
 Indeed, it is for your sake
that all things are ordered,
  so that,
as the abounding grace of God
 is shared by more and more,
  the greater may be
   the chorus of thanksgiving
that ascends to the glory of God.
No wonder we do not lose heart!
Though our outward humanity is
 in decay, yet day by day
  we are inwardly renewed.
Our troubles are slight
 and short lived;
and their outcome an eternal
 glory which outweighs them far.
Meanwhile our eyes are fixed,
 not on the things that are seen,
but on the things that are unseen:
for what is seen passes away;
 what is unseen is eternal.
For we know that
if the earthly frame that houses us
 today should be demolished,
  we possess a building
   which God has provided —
a house not made by human hands,
 eternal, and in heaven.
In this present body we do indeed
 groan; we yearn to have
  our heavenly habitation
   put on over this one... CORINTHIANS 4:7–5:2 NEB

Clay Pots or Flower Vases?

In Bible times many kinds of containers were made from clay. Today simple red clay pots are made to hold plants. These pots don't cost much because they are fired in the kiln without particular care. Often they become marred, scratched, or cracked. The value of this particular kind of pot is questionable. If it becomes cracked, it may simple be marked "Damaged . . . N.G." A pot in this condition might be placed on a shelf in a greenhouse—segregated, isolated, rejected, used only in great necessity.

A fine china vessel is much more appealing to the eye. Its ornamentation, its fine porcelain finish, and the care with which it must be hand-fired make it much more admirable. This type of vessel is looked for. People are eager to own it. They appreciate the craftsmanship that is exhibited in its fine details.

But suppose we examine a certain common clay pot more closely and notice that it contains a small object. We remove it and discover that it is a precious jewel—a pearl of great price. Immediately the clay pot becomes much more valuable. We desire to own it . . . not for the clay pot itself, but for the precious stone. People who know the secret that the clay pot holds can now display it without apology or shame; they care for it, they guard it, they protect it from harm.

The clay pot is like the stone that the builders rejected; yet it became the chief cornerstone. Today people continue to have the clay-pot attitude toward handicapped people. But parents of a handicapped child recognize their child's real value. They know the secret that within him or her there is the bright glow of love.

So, like the apostle, we parents continue on the arduous course God has marked out for us. Like St. Paul we suffer all kinds of difficulties. They get us down at times, but our faith in Christ keeps us from being overwhelmed by them. We keep looking toward "our heavenly habitation," where all of us Christians—including our precious handicapped child—will live forever in inexpressible joy.

As a parent
   of a mentally retarded son,
I can say that every day he is,
   in a sense,
a source of embarrassment to me.
   Every day
      my pride and self conceit
are peeled away layer by layer.
   Every day
      I stand naked before men.
Every day
      the sophistication of society
   that I would like to maintain
is shattered before my eyes.
   I feel alone and lonely.

   yet I love my son;
      I call him my own.
      I know that I need him
as much as he needs me.
   with my love
I stand in relationship to him
   as Christ with his love
stands in relationship to me.
   Every day
I am a source of embarrassment
   to Christ.
      Every day
         Christ, who would glory
            in His Creation,
stands embarrassed by my wrongs.
         Every day,
   Christ who formed me,
as the pinnacle of His Creation,
      sees my fallen estate,
yet He loves me. This I know.
Amen. Amen. "Come Lord Jesus!"

83